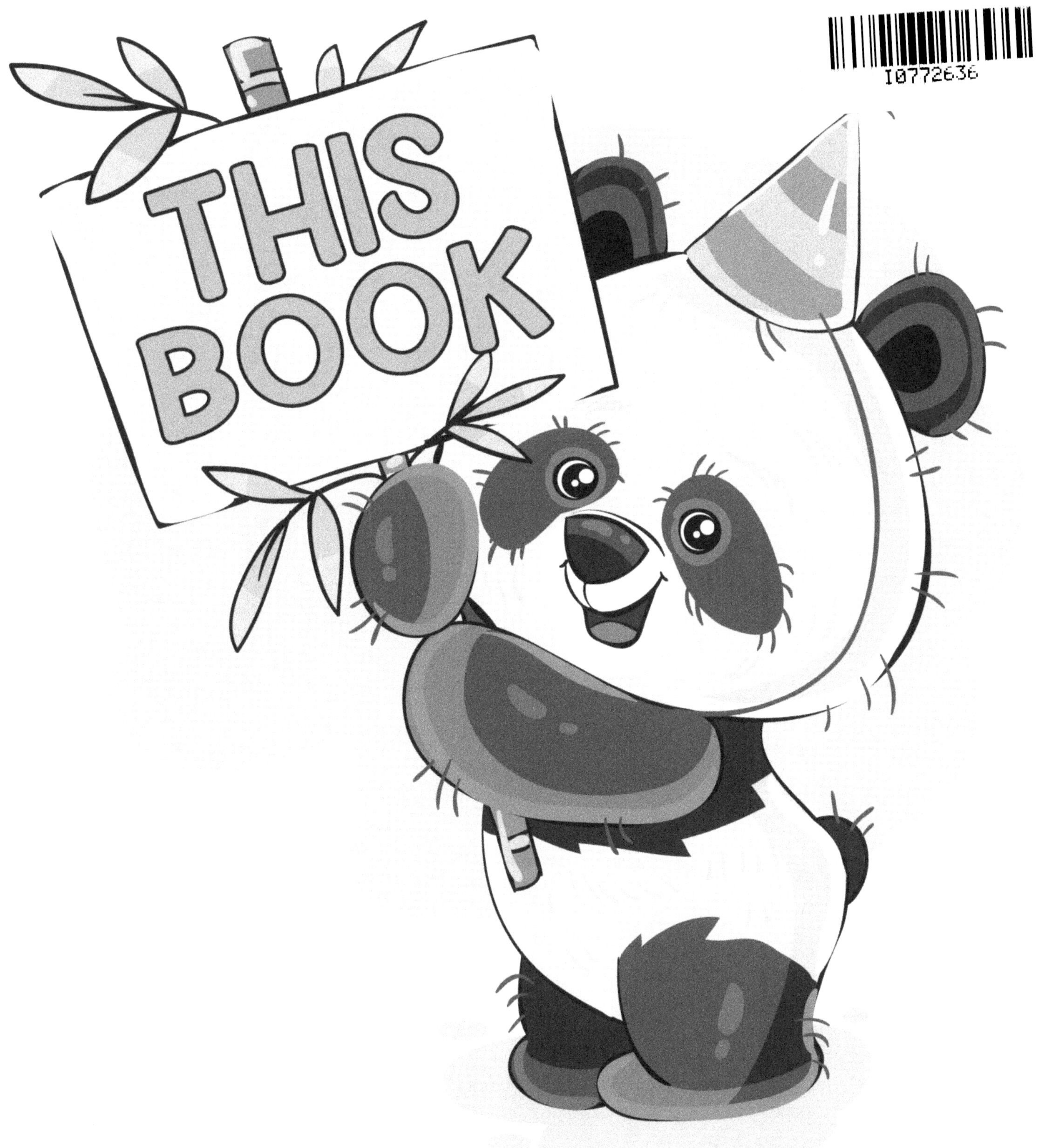
THIS
BOOK
BELONGS TO.....

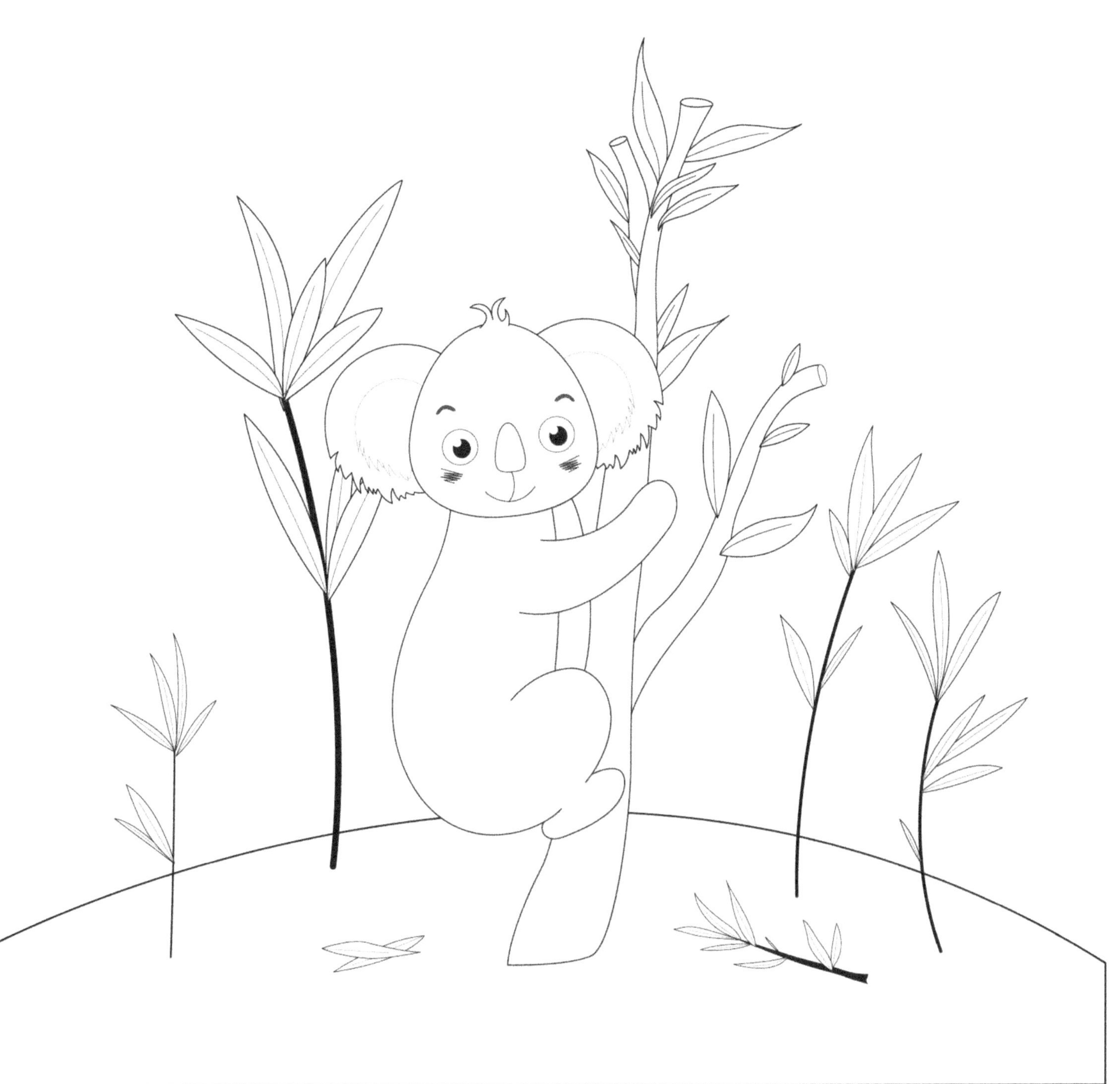

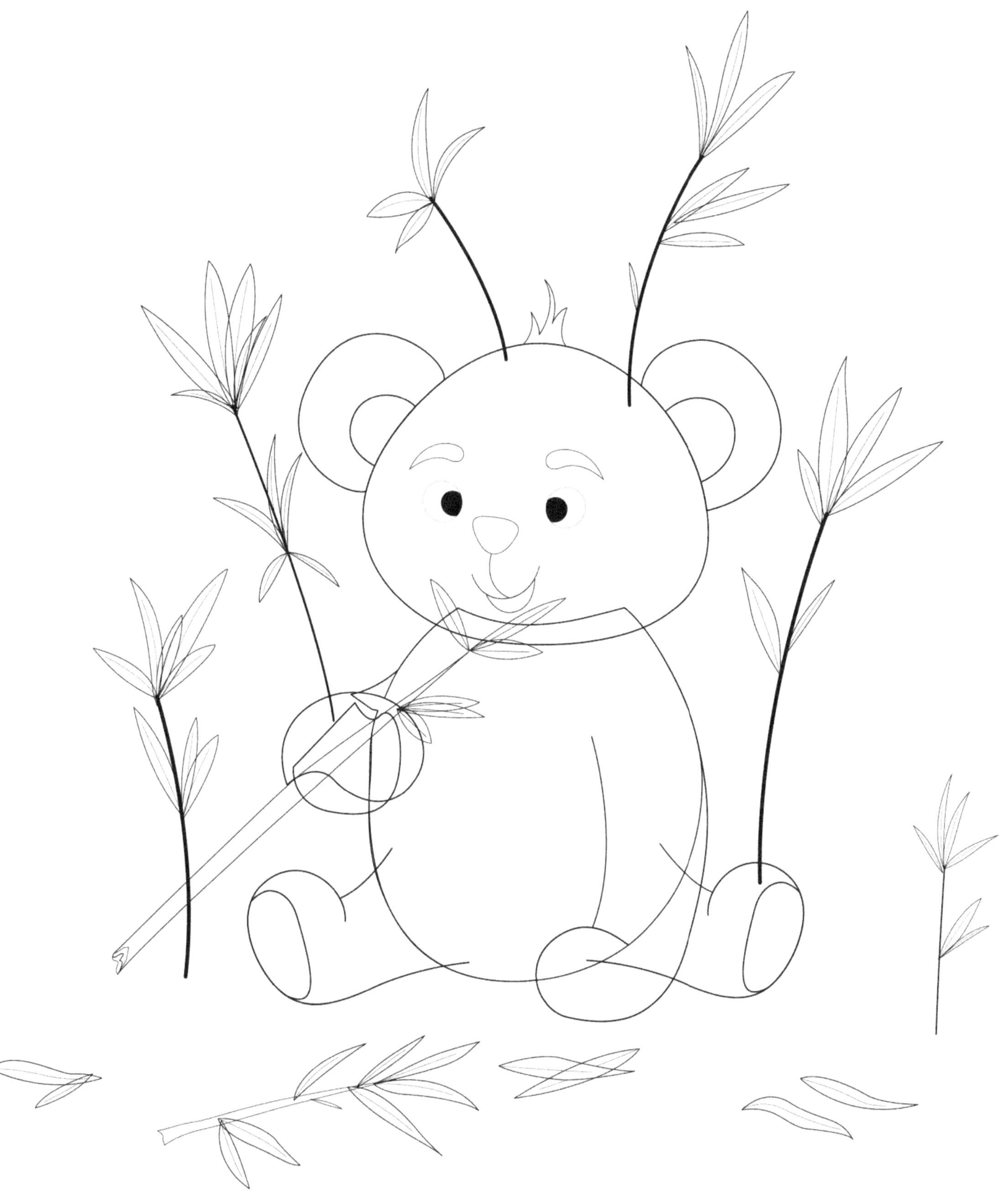

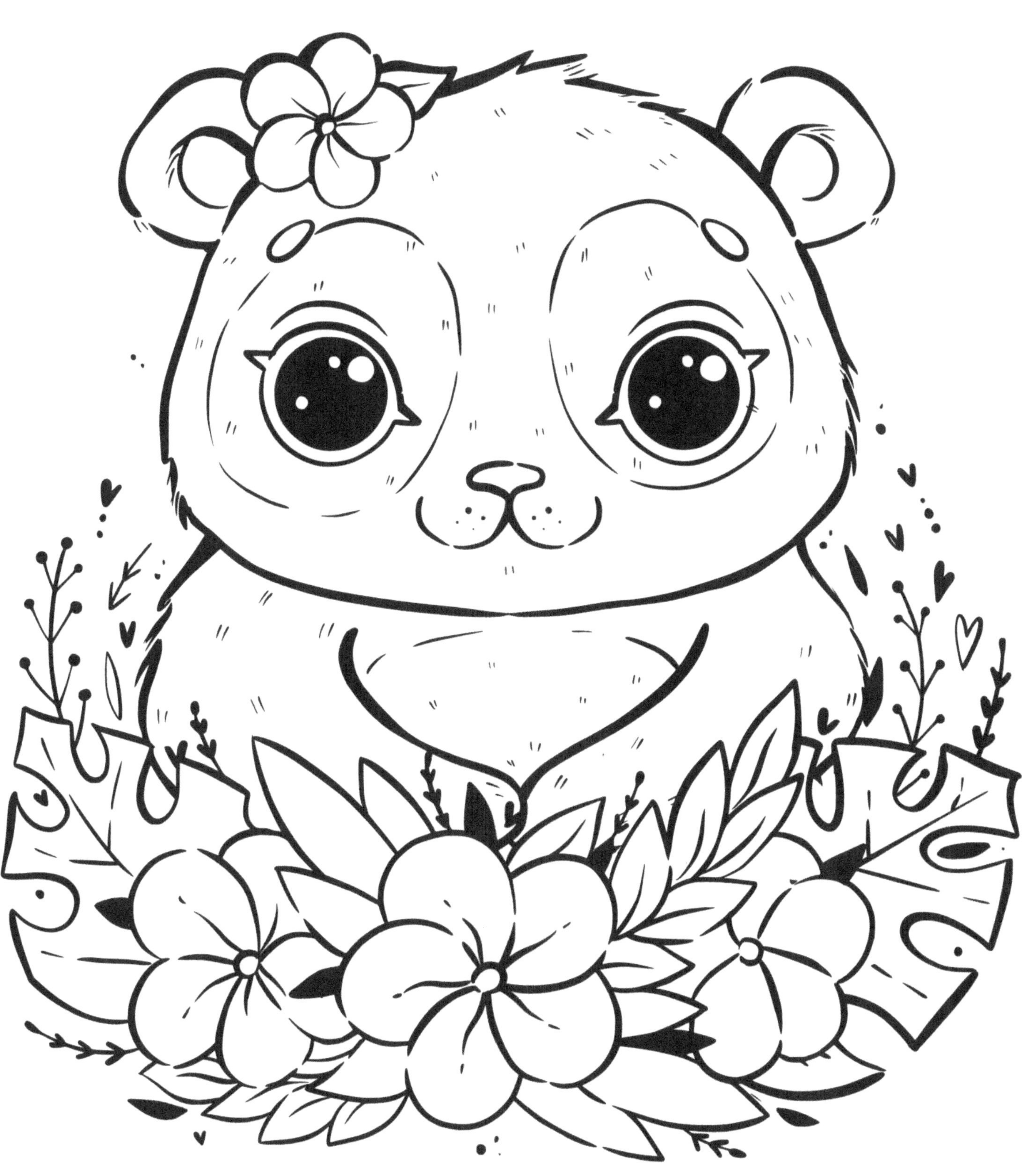

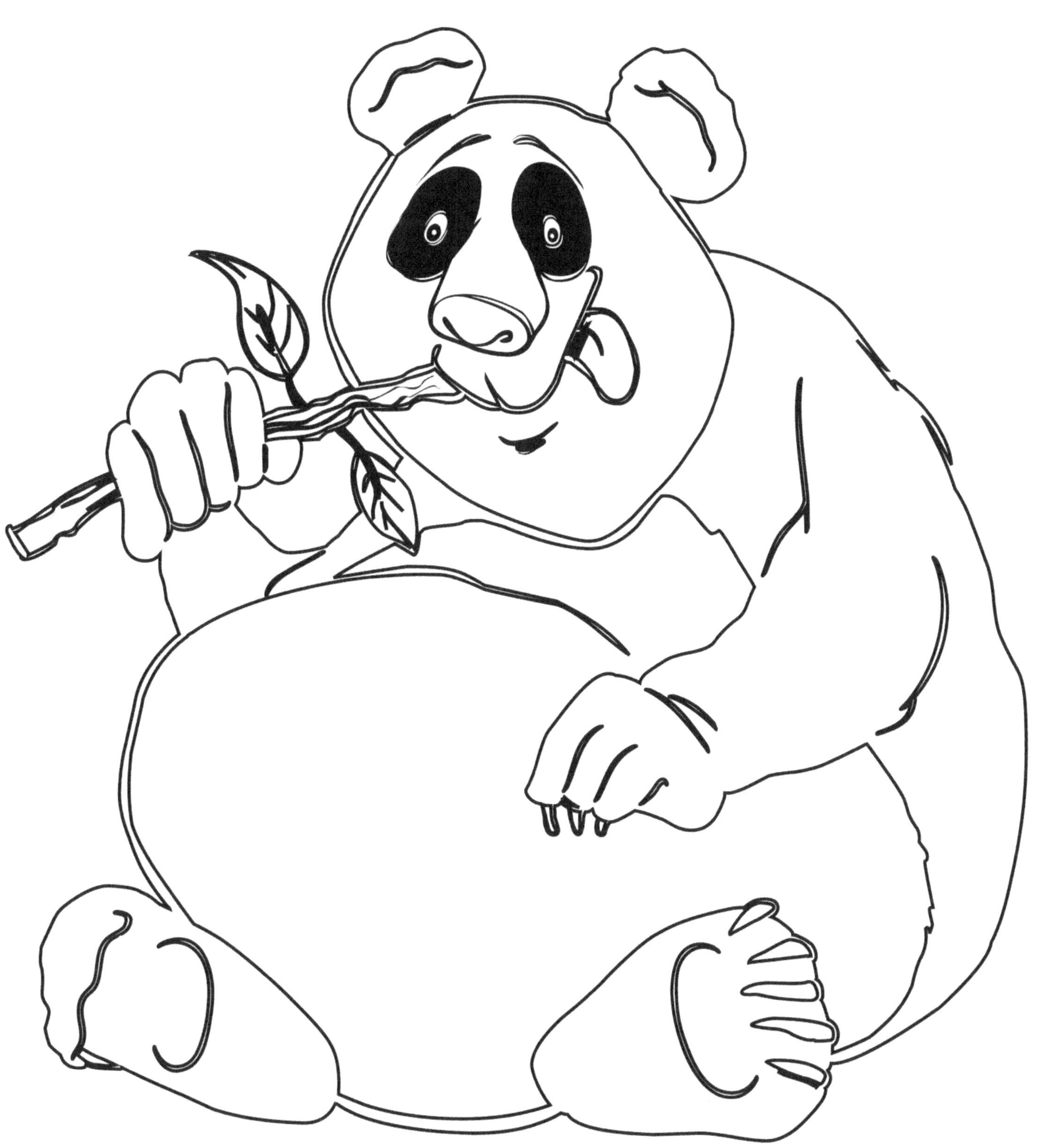

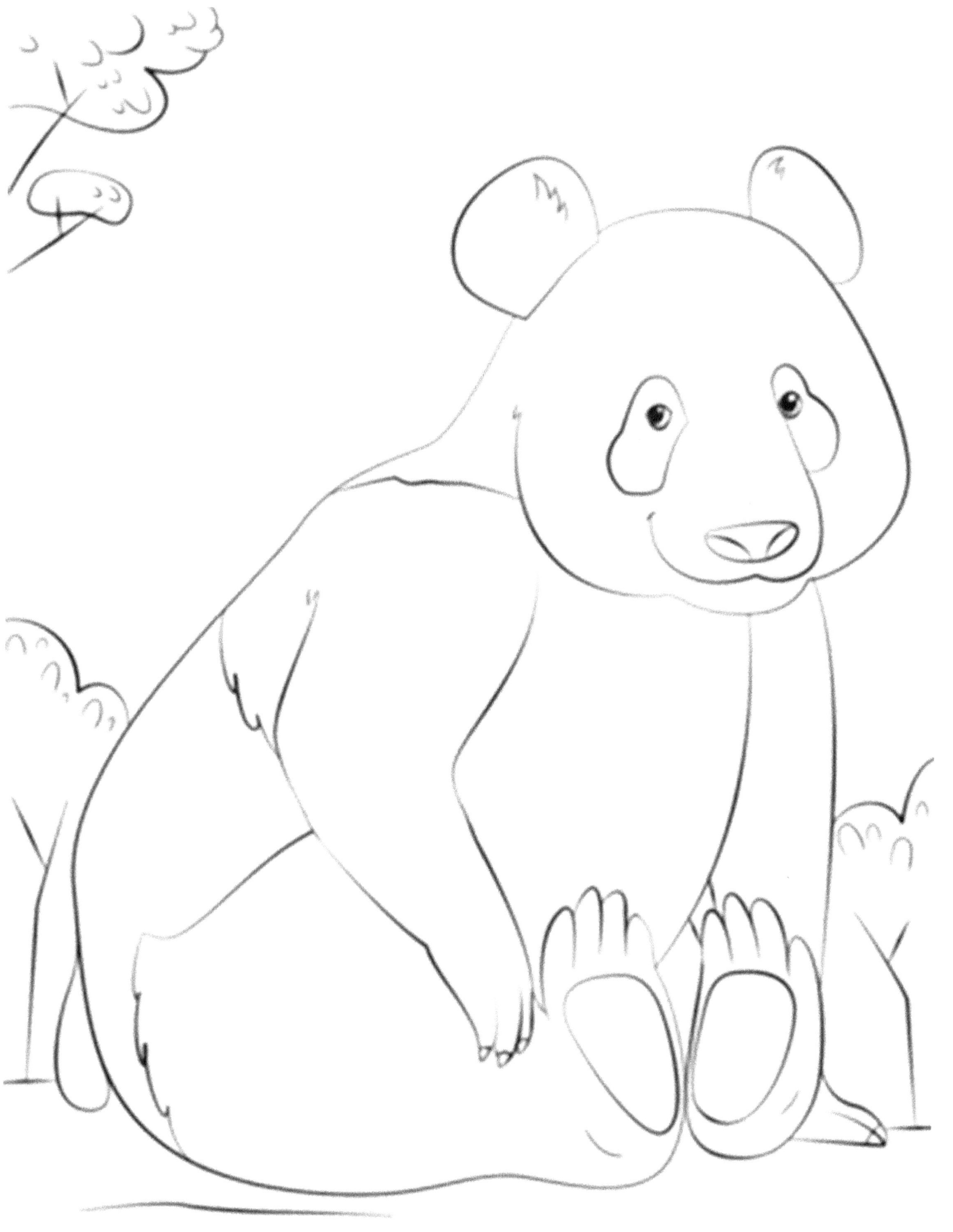

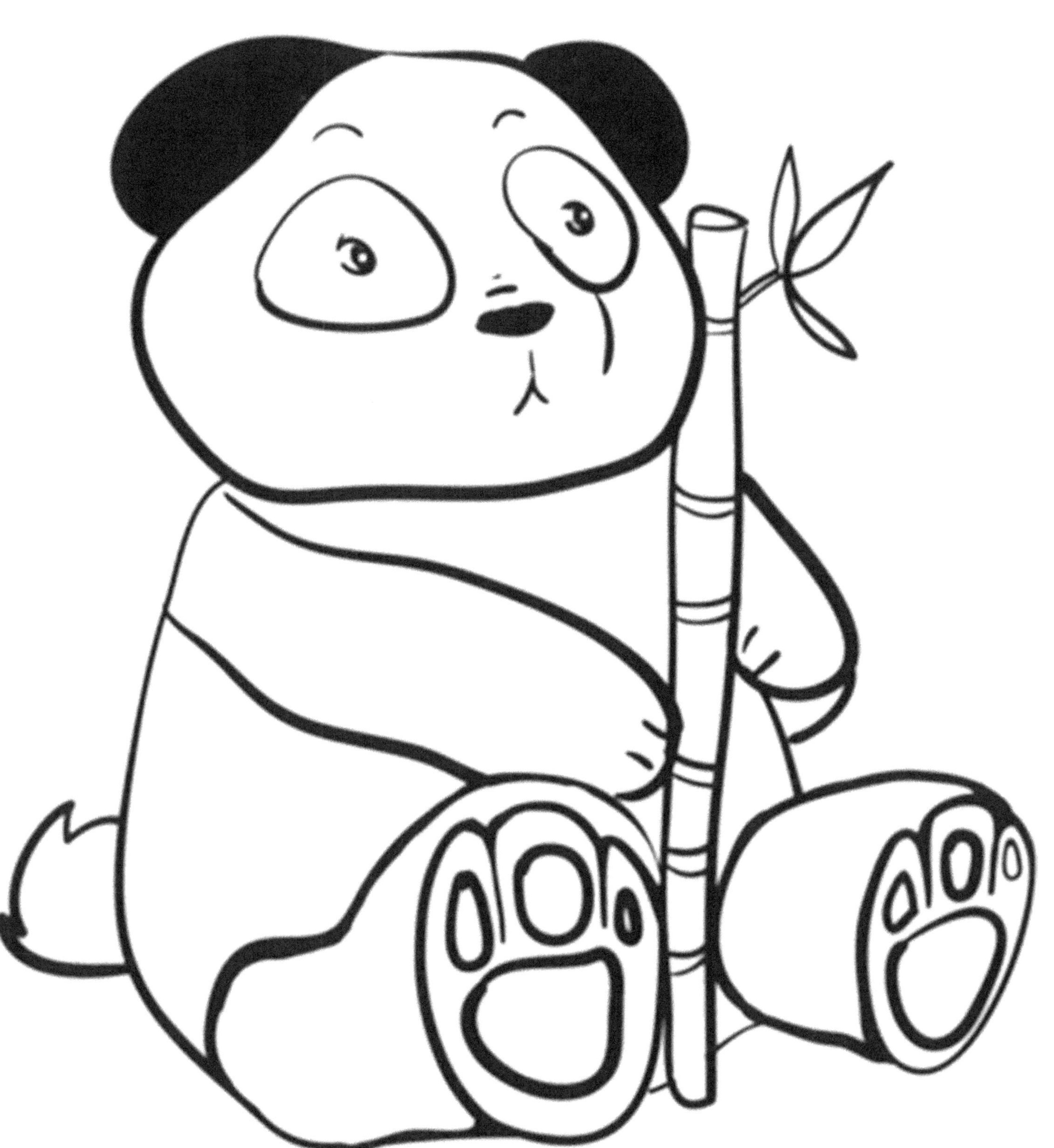

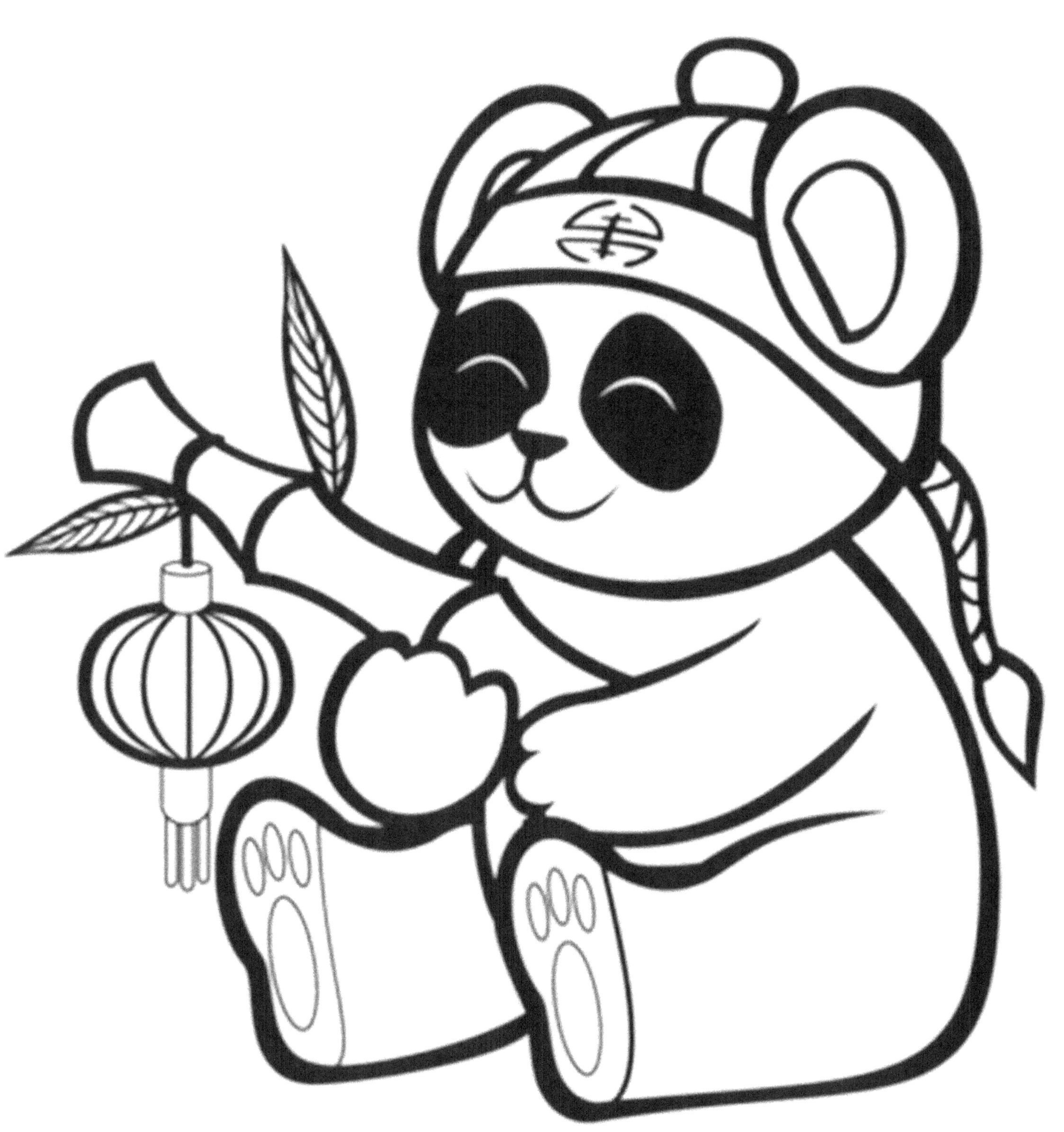

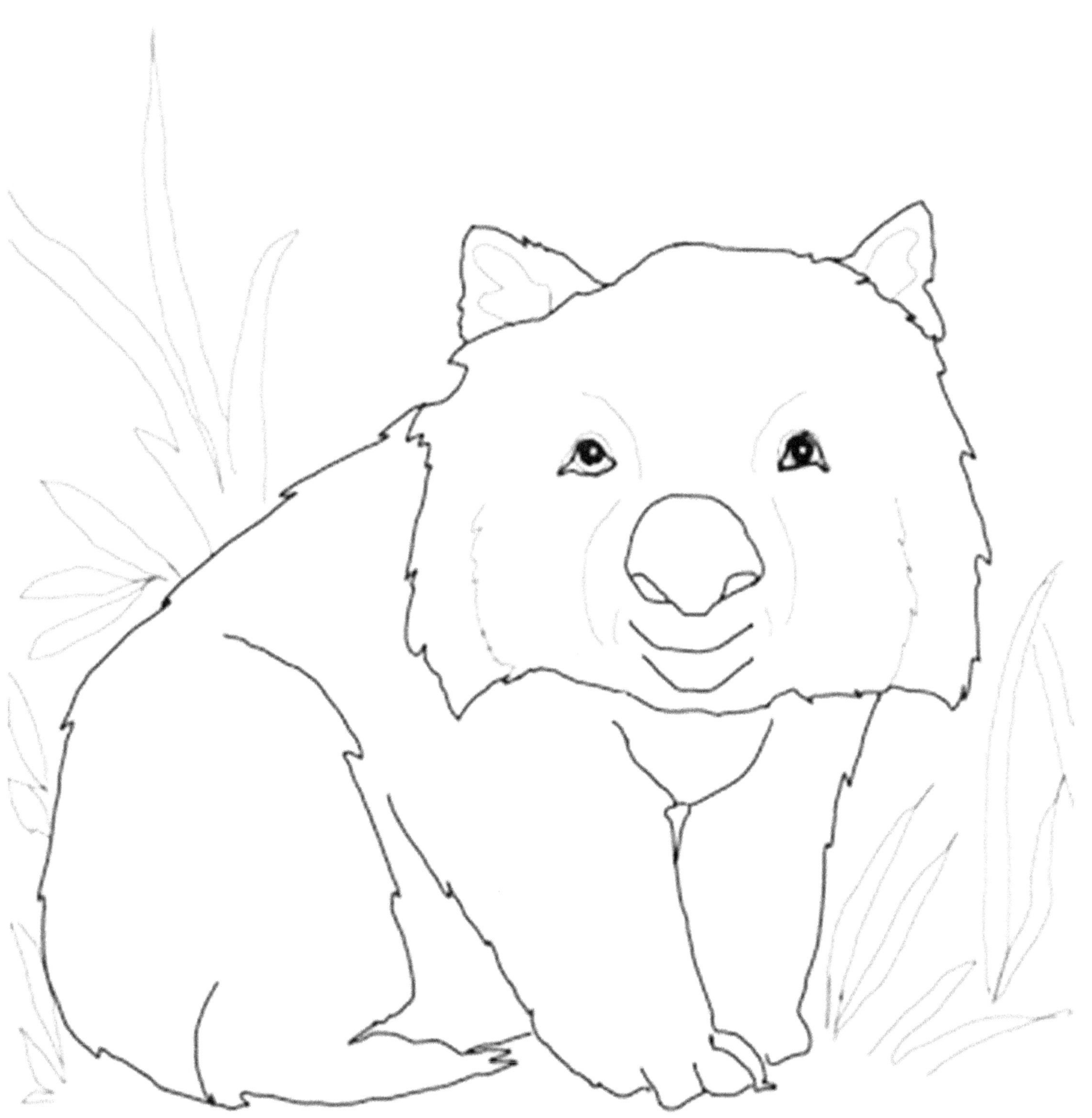

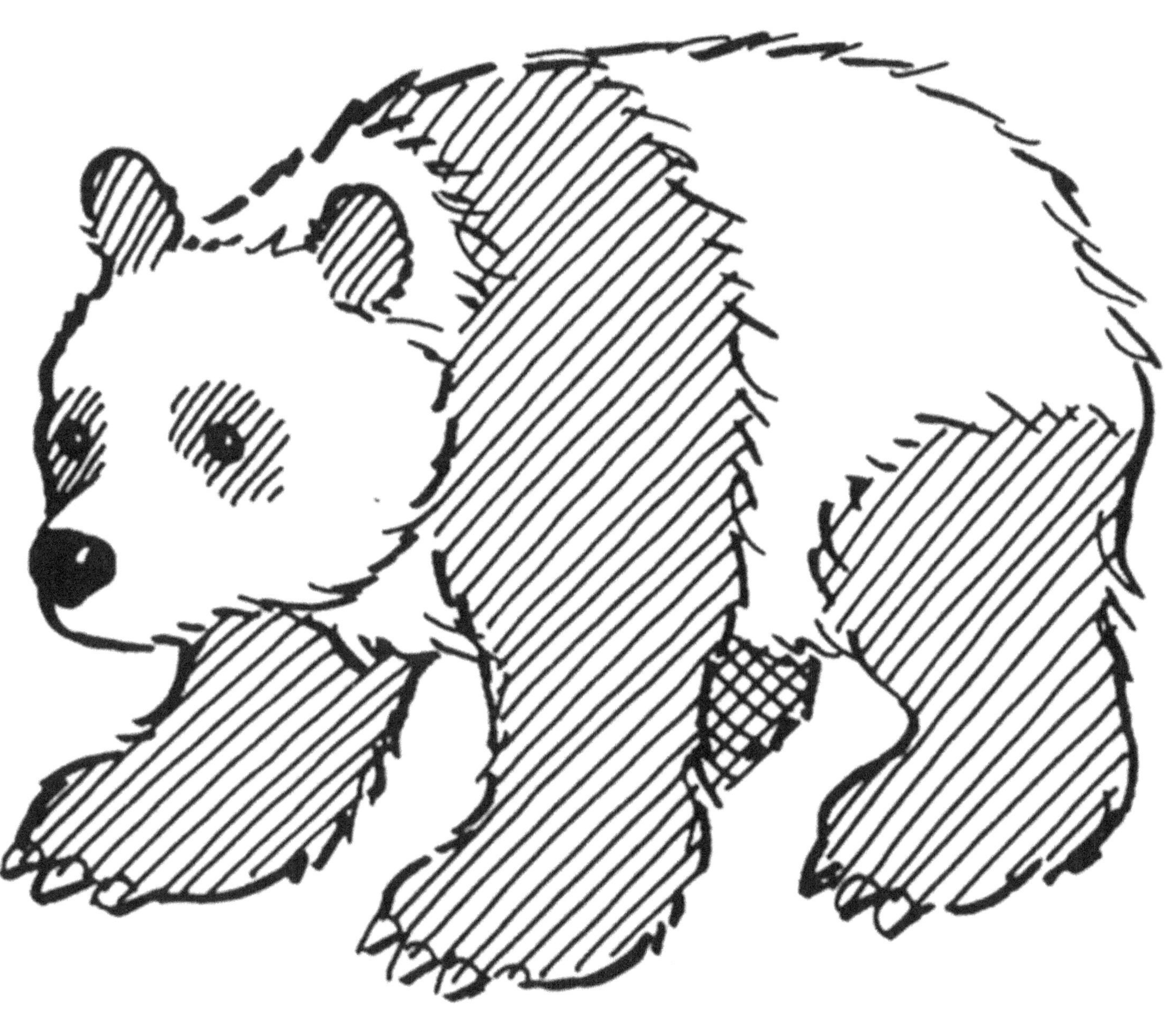

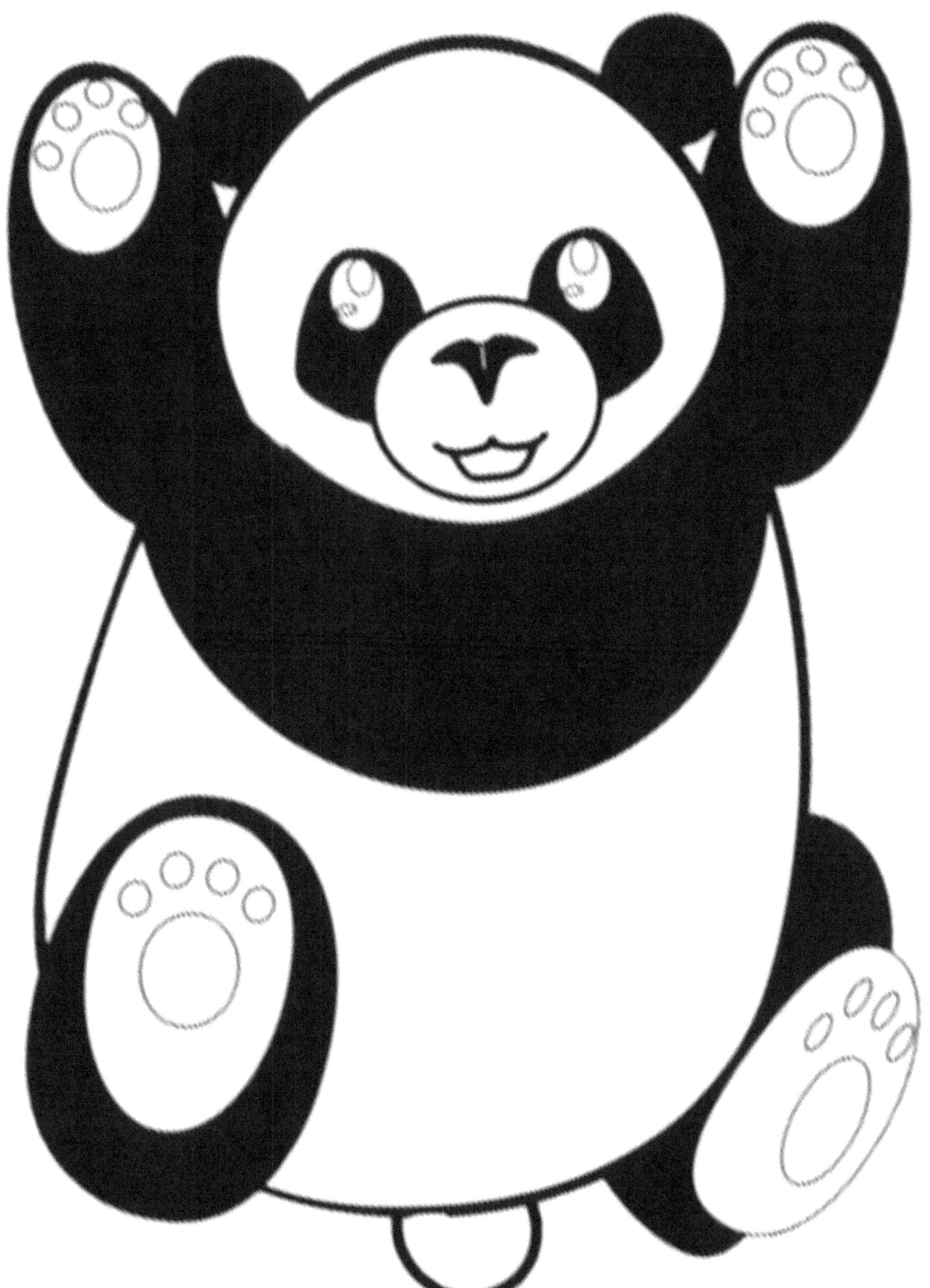

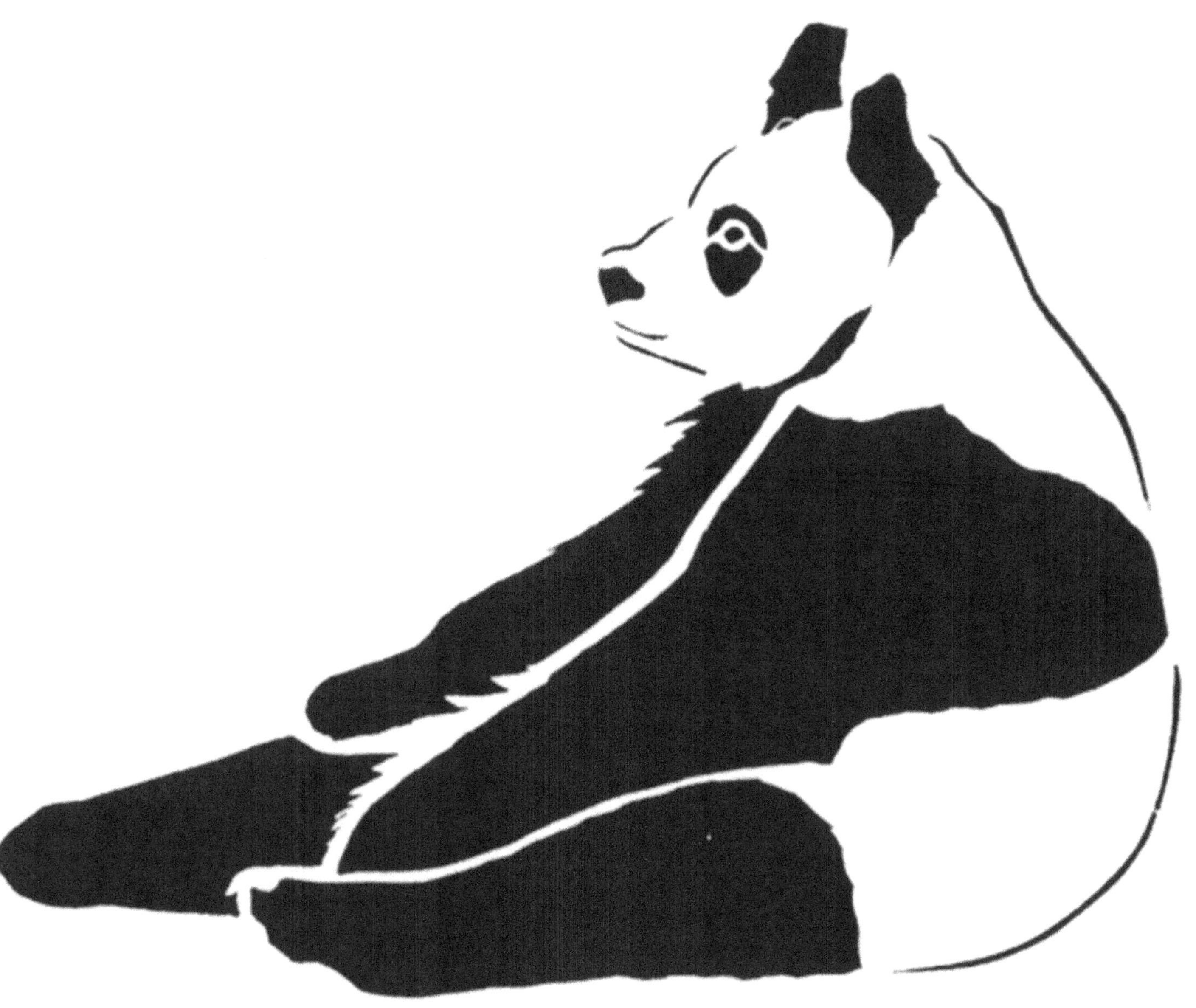

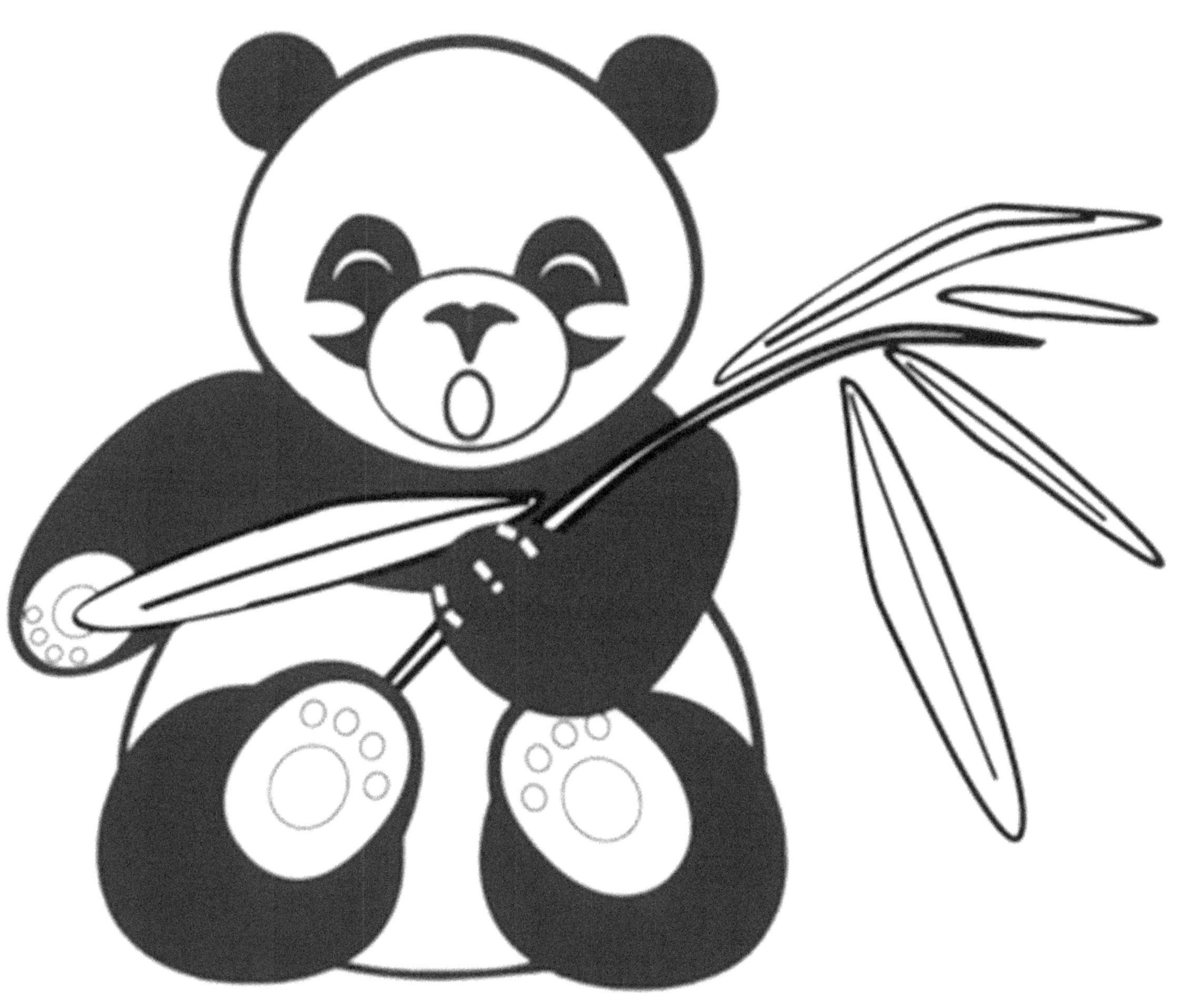

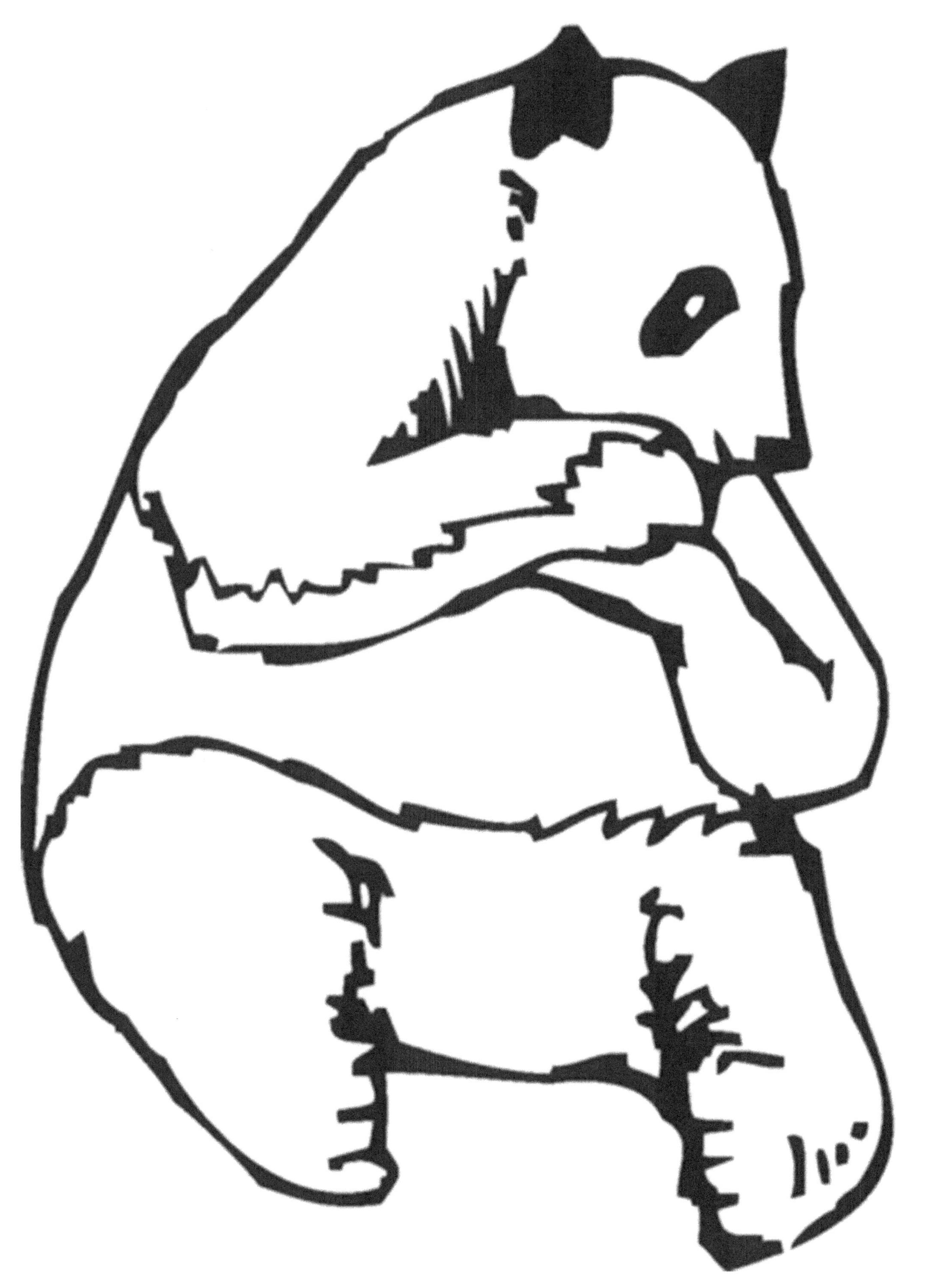

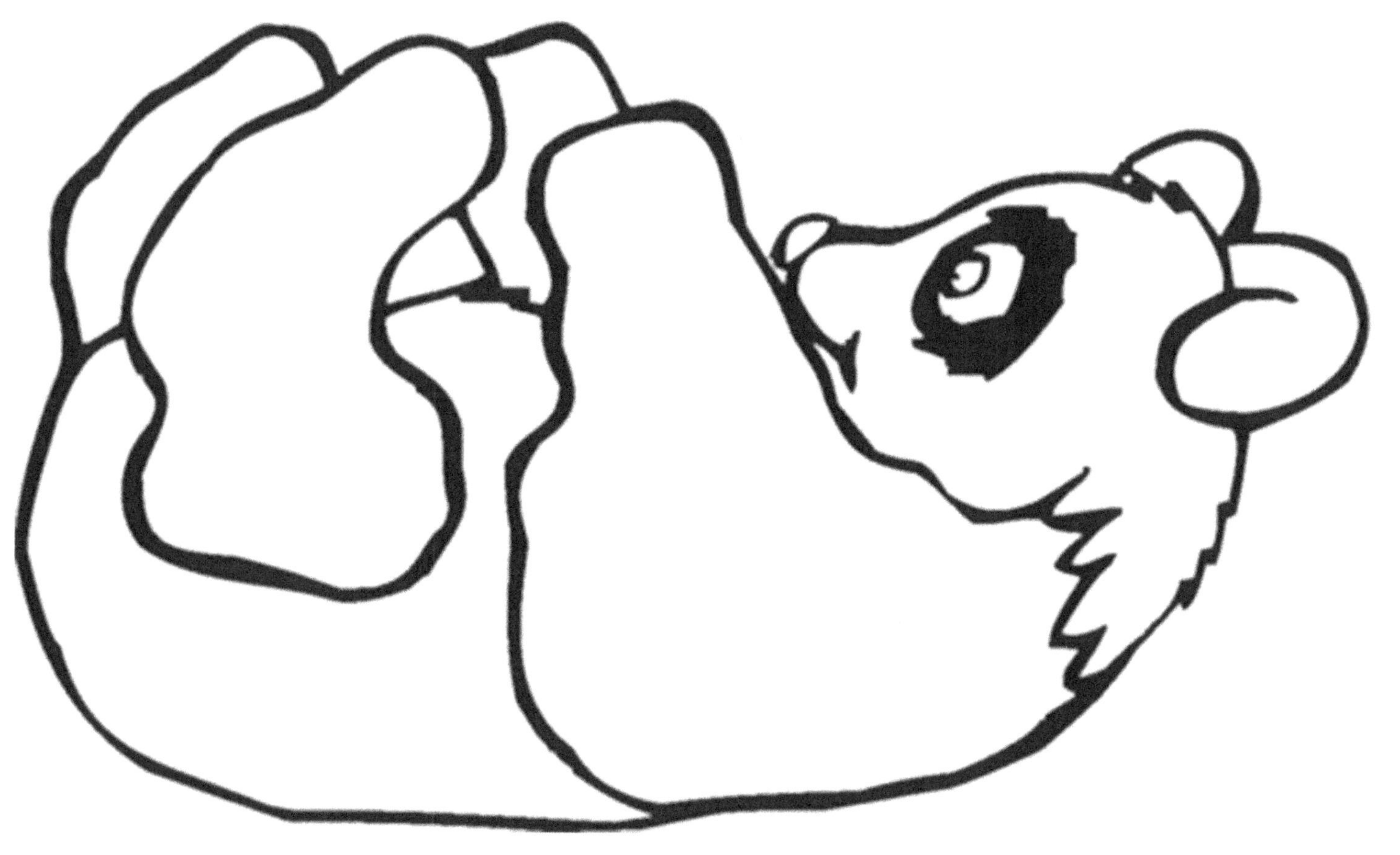

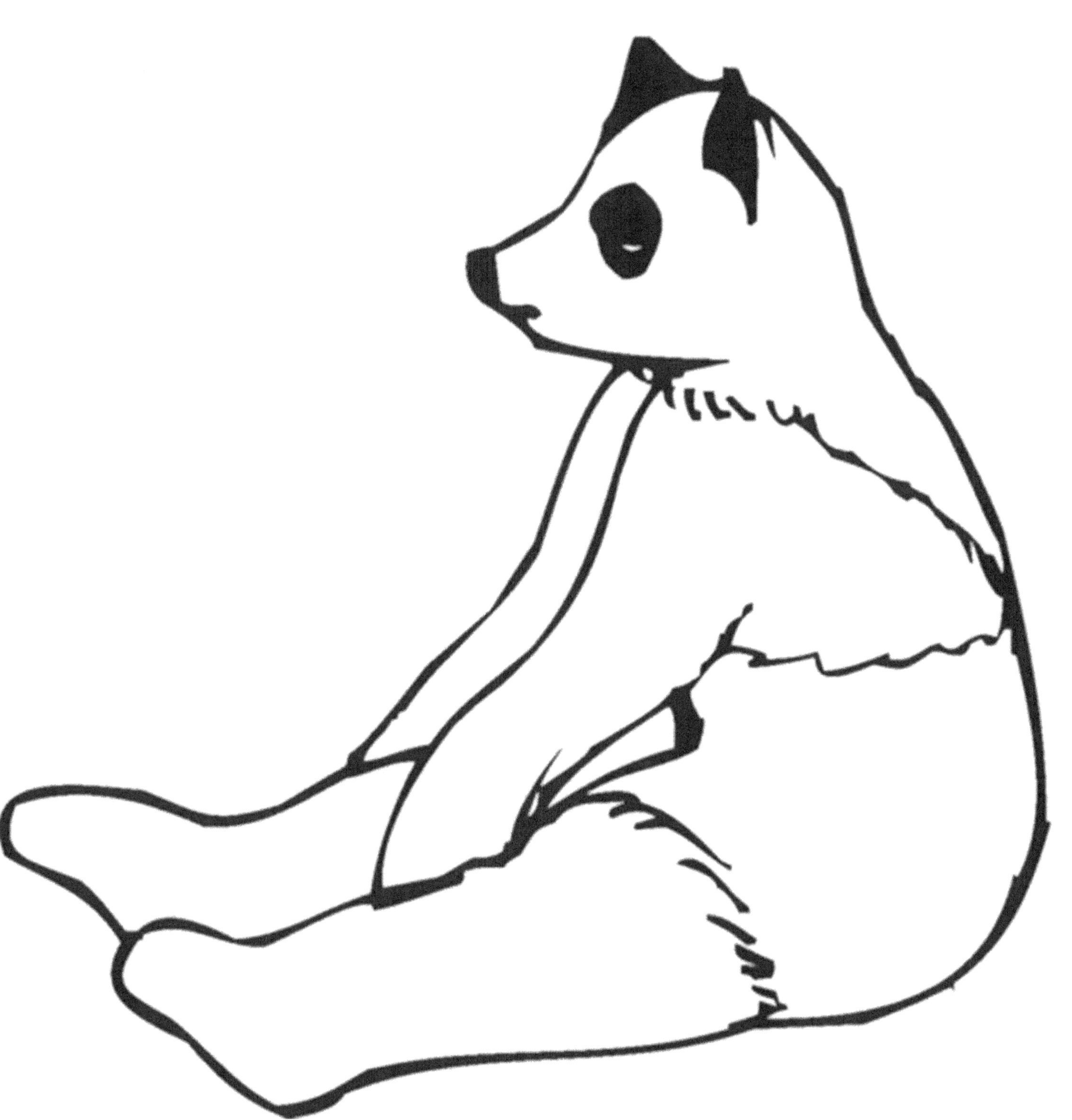

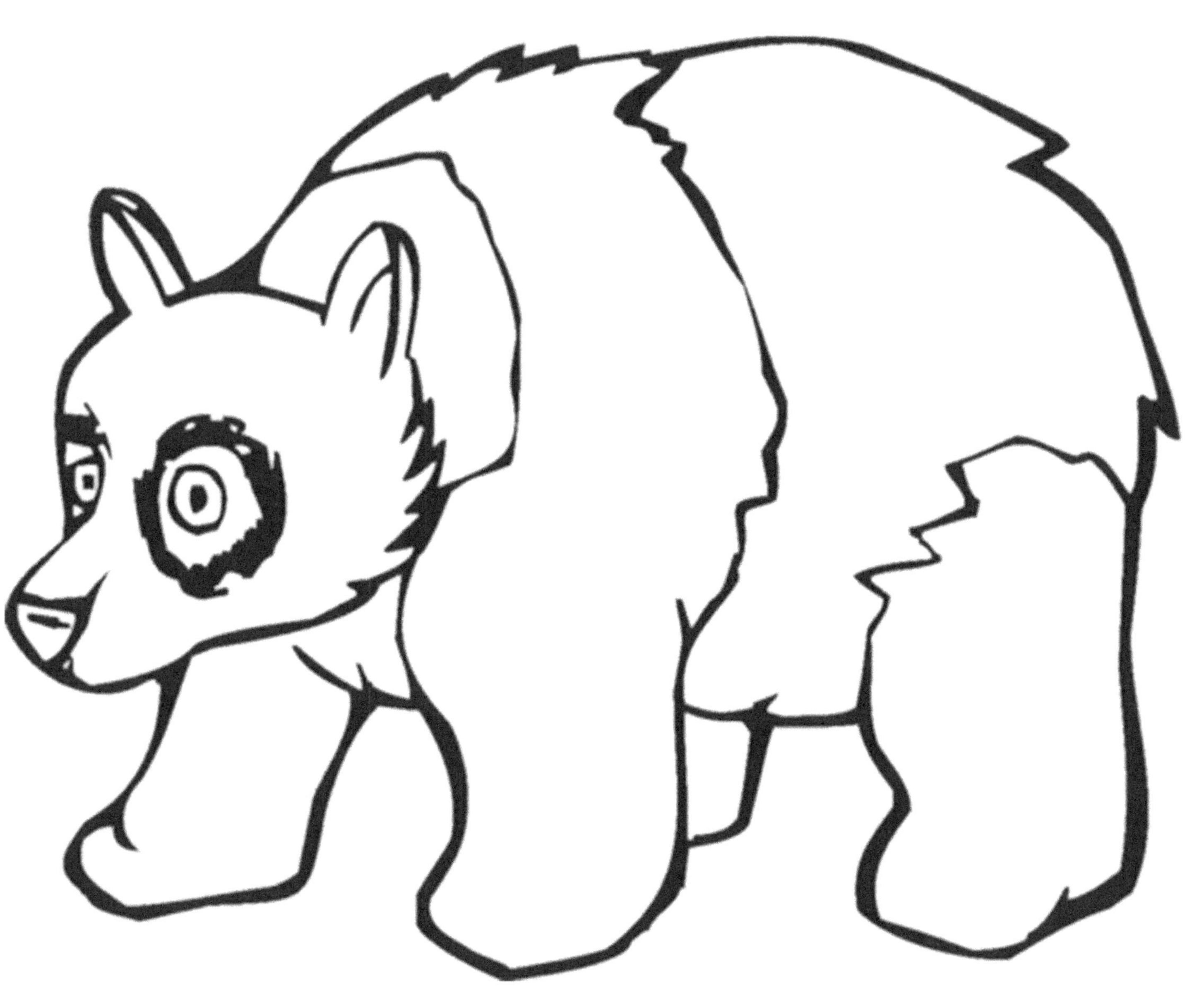

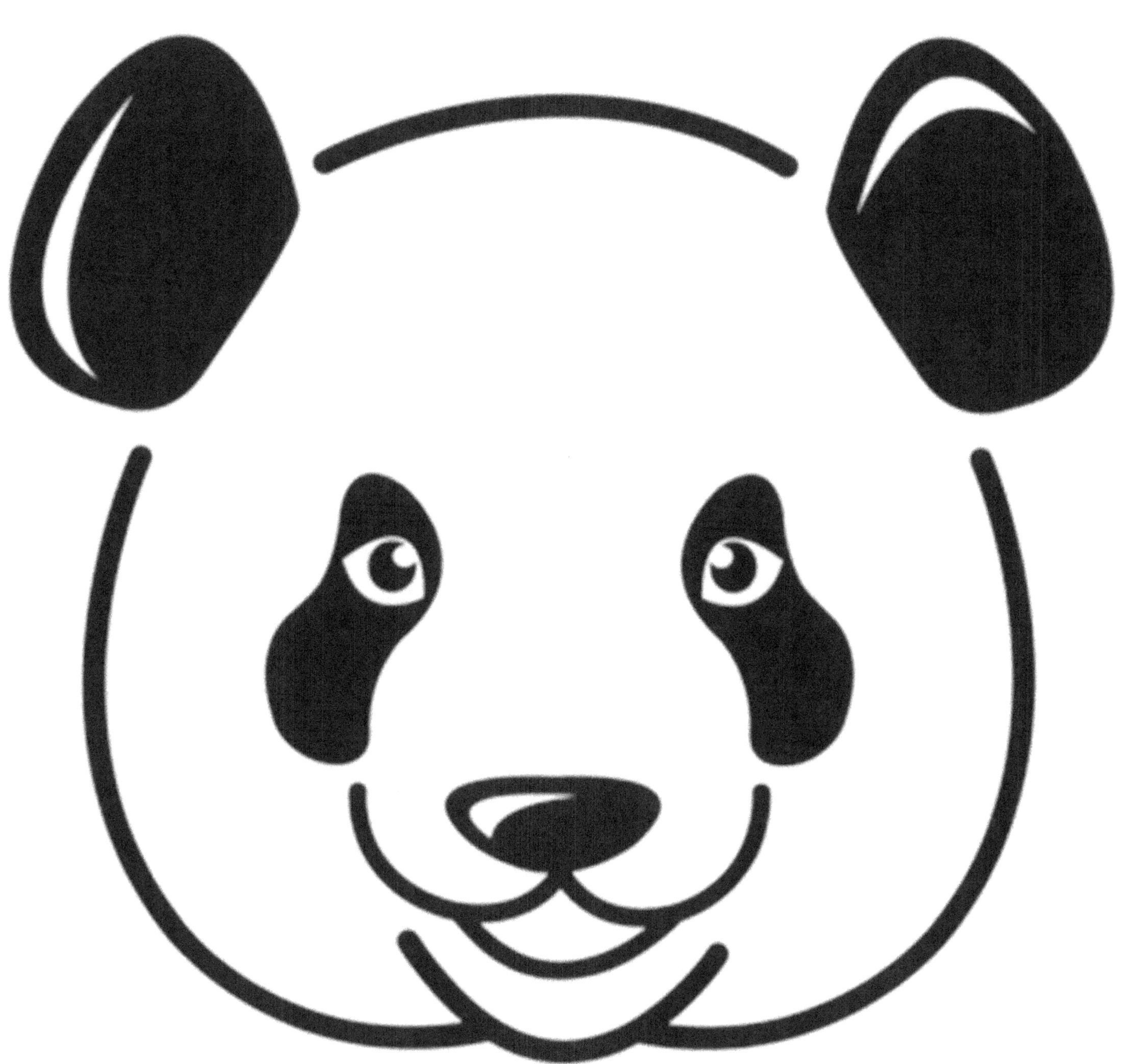

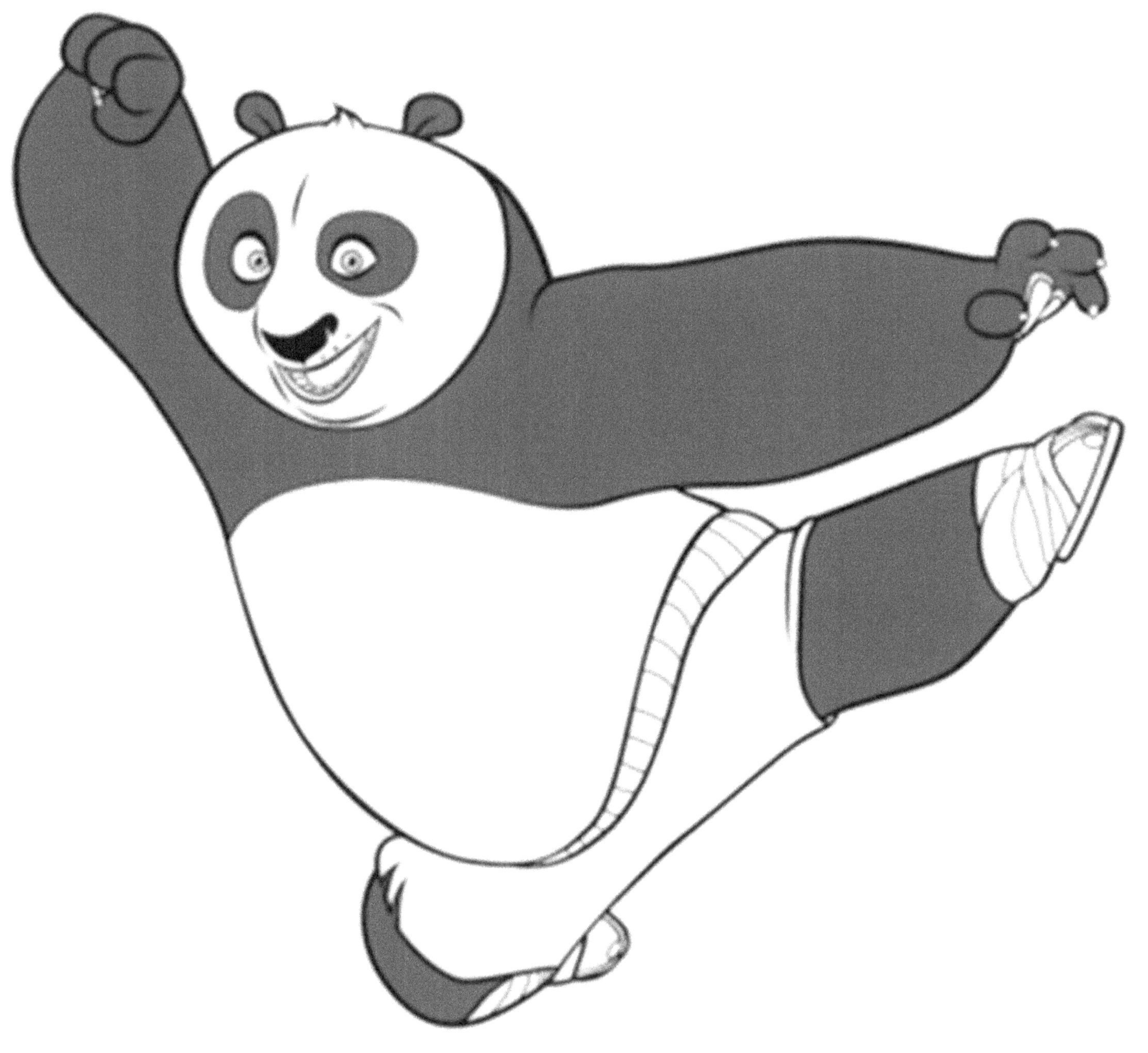

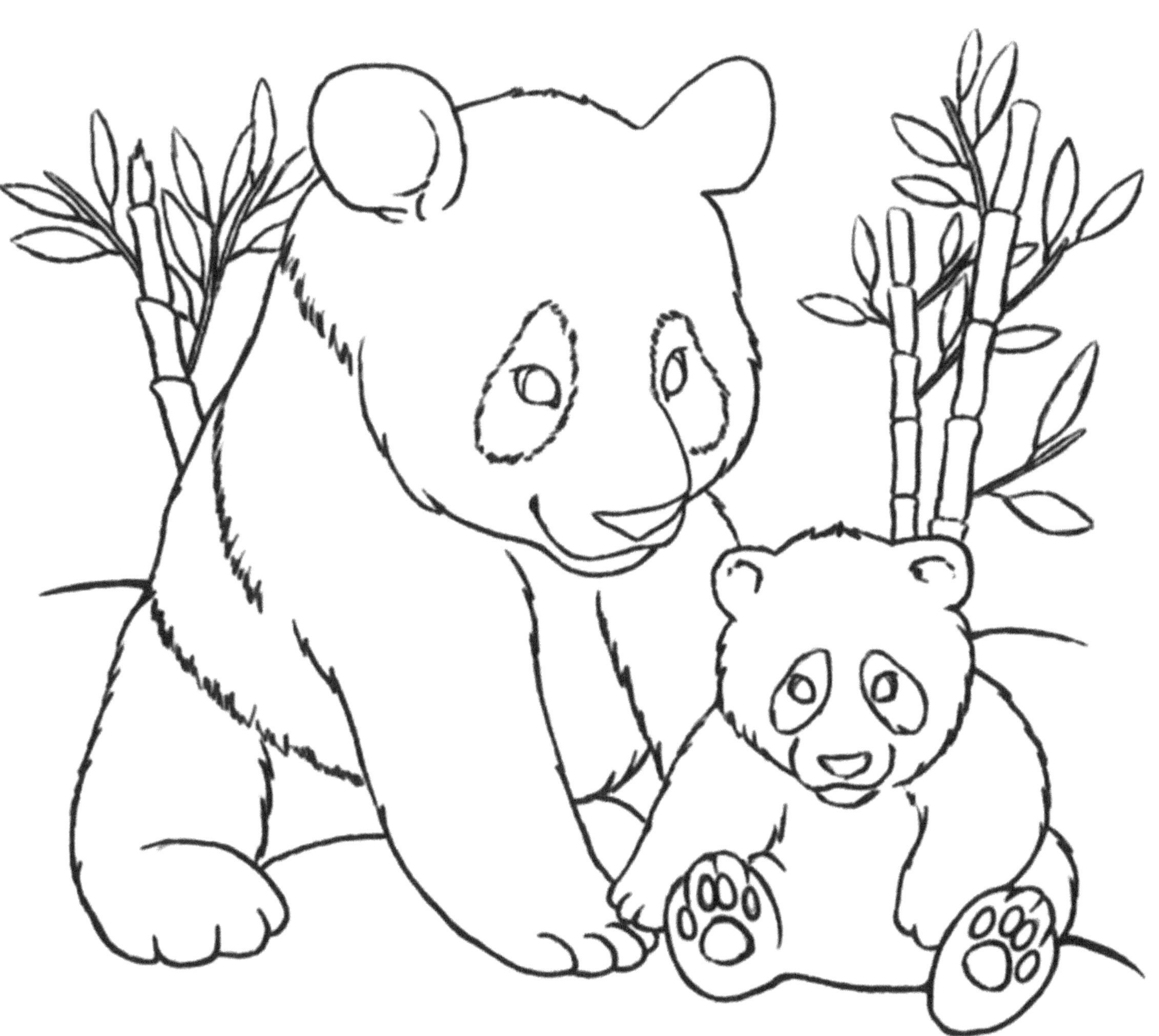

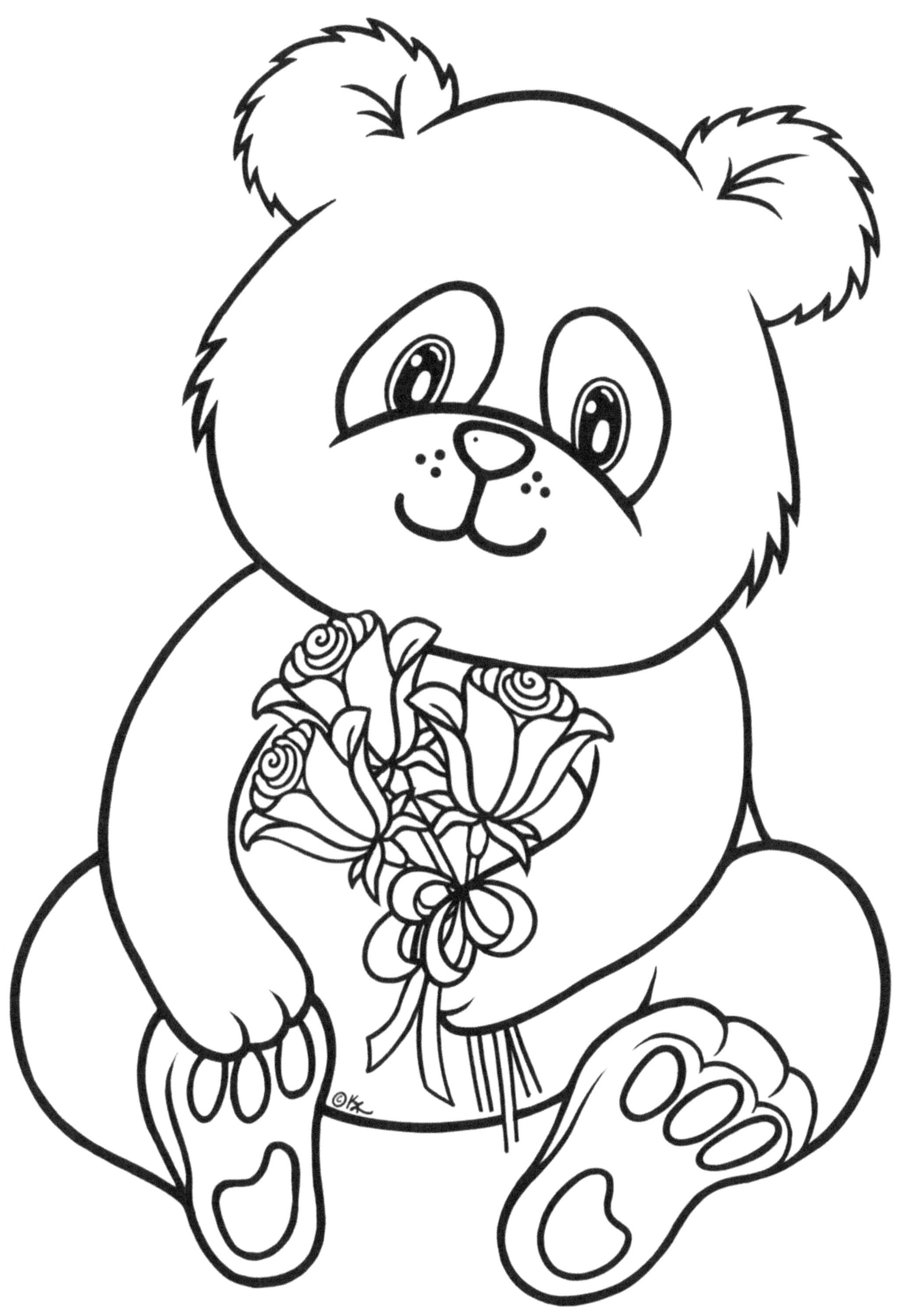

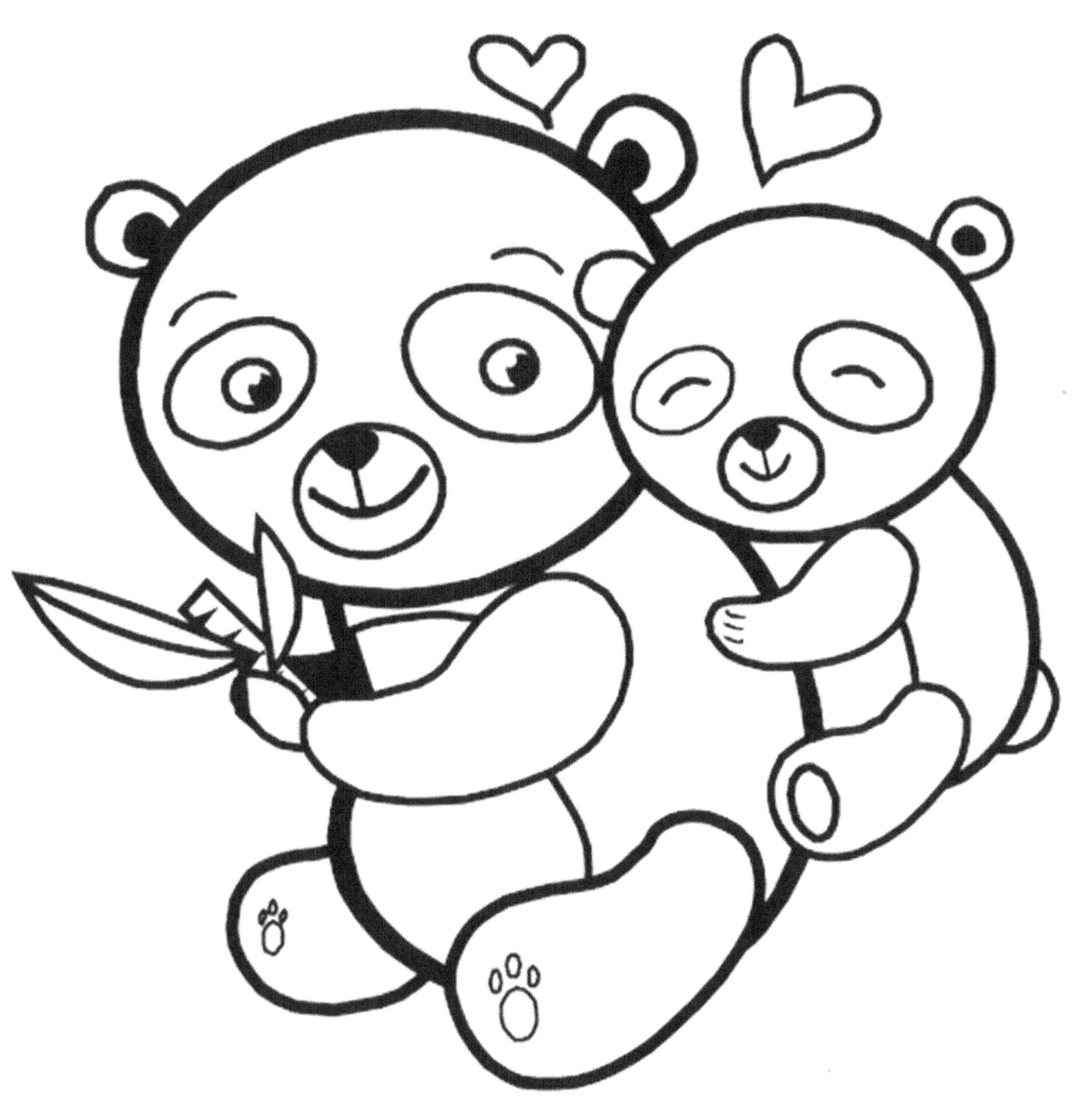

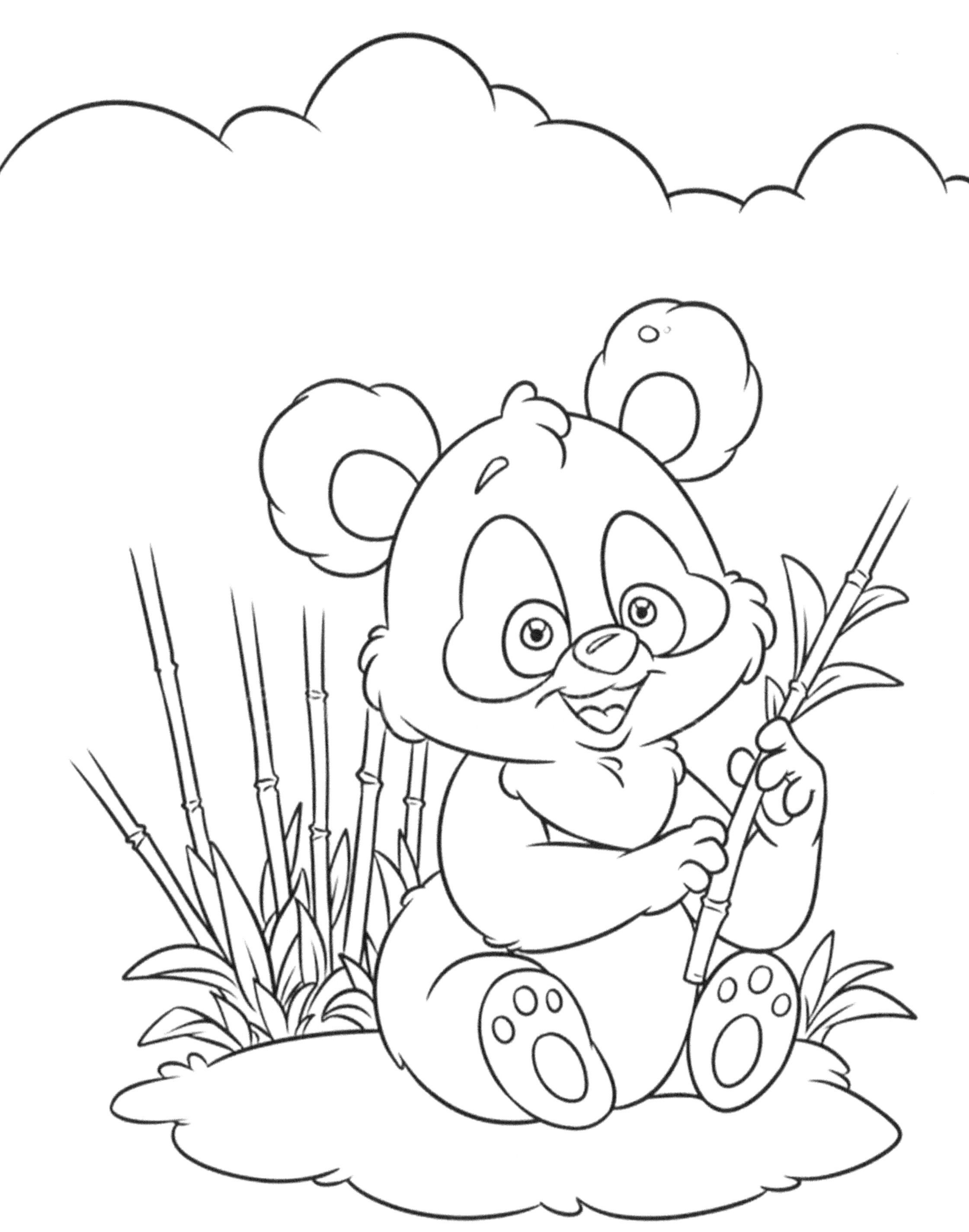

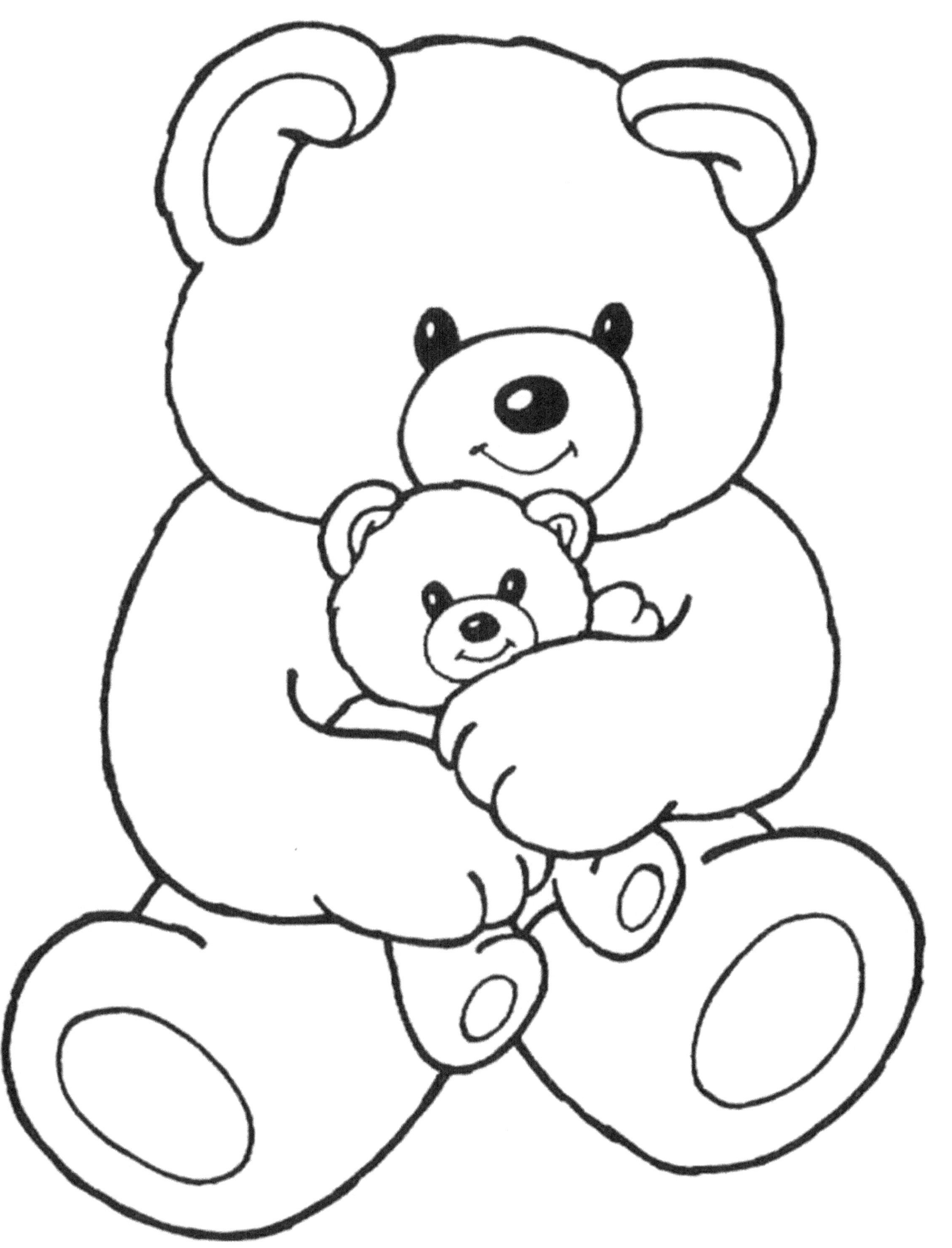

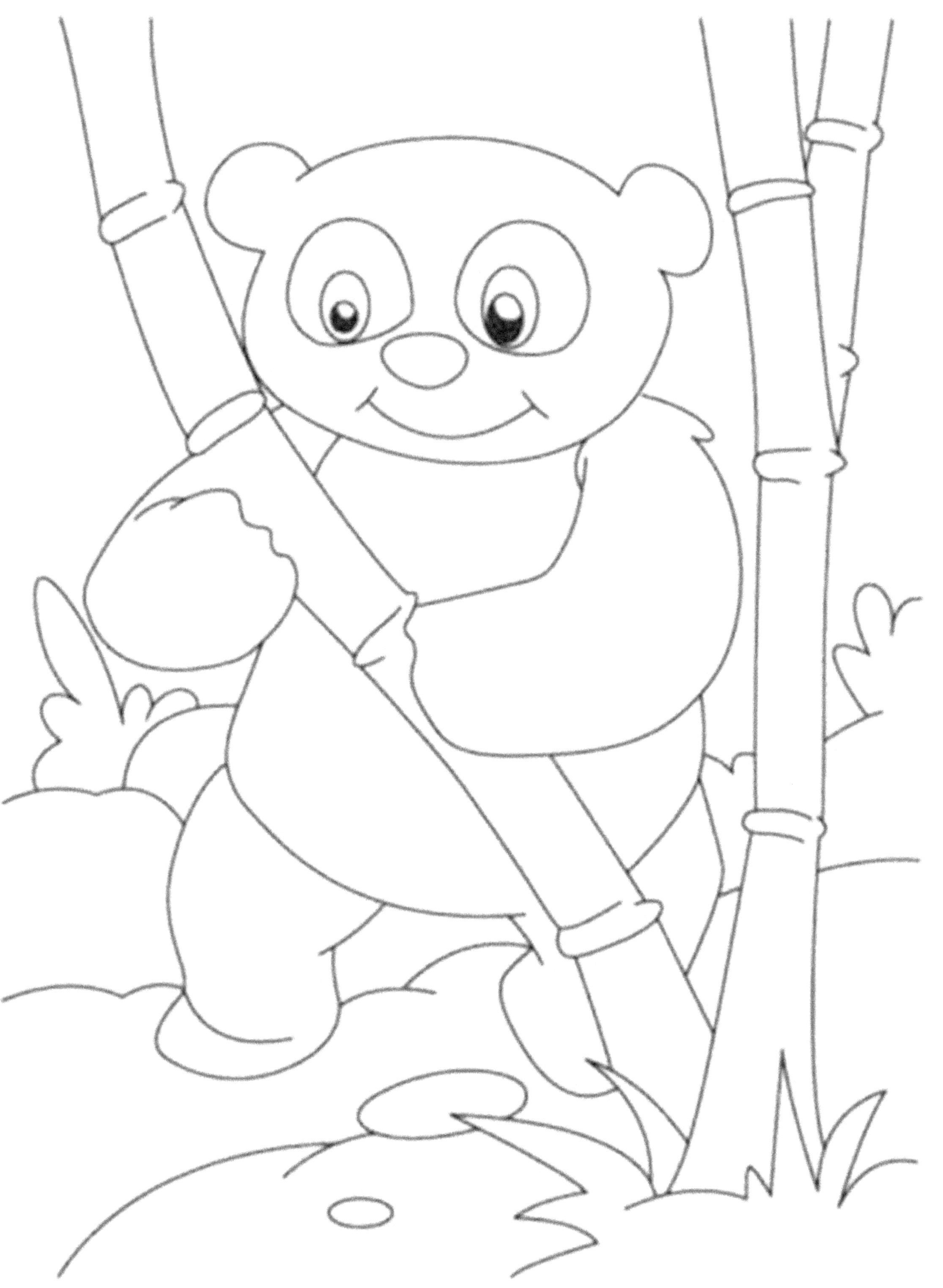